Nettles

Nettles   POEMS BY
BETTY ADCOCK

LOUISIANA STATE UNIVERSITY PRESS
BATON ROUGE AND LONDON
1983

Designer: Barbara Werden
Typeface: Linotron Bembo
Typesetter: G&S Typesetters, Inc.

LIBRARY OF CONGRESS CATALOGING IN PUBLICATION DATA

Adcock, Betty.
  Nettles.

  I. Title.
PS3551.D396N4   1983   811'.54   83-726
ISBN 0-8071-1101-5
ISBN 0-8071-1103-1 (pbk.)

Grateful acknowledgment is made to the following publications in which some of
these poems originally appeared, sometimes under different titles or in different
versions: *Kentucky Poetry Review, Pembroke Magazine, Georgia Review, Plainsong,
Lyricist, Southern Poetry Review, Green River Review, Cedar Rock, Uzzano, South
Carolina Review, Applachian Review, Kenyon Review, ASFA Quarterly.*
  Italicized lines in the poem titled "Lines on a Poet's Face" are from poems by
Robert Penn Warren, *Selected Poems, 1923–1974* (Random House), copyright
© 1976 by Robert Penn Warren. By permission of Random House.

Louisiana Paperback Edition, 1983

99 98 97 96 95 94 93 92 91 90   5 4 3 2

For Guy Owen
1925–1981

Contents

PART FOUR

Part
 ONE

South Woods in October, with the Spiders of Memory

There's no touch like this one
except (if you remember it) your baptism,
that silent passage through breaking
unbreathable circles of light
where you were caught quaking and brief
in the fingers of clarity.

The world's strung with embraces.

And this air is pearled with a music
far from us but earth-struck
and deep as that water
from which you could wake and wake.

You can never quite see what makes it
to echo and thrum with the taken.

There's just this touch that is not
like a lover's, is more
barely moth dust and sun slant,
your eyes new-lashed with it.
You go forward by shudder and wreckage,
bearer of imperceptible message,
brushing the small dead from your face.

Hand Made

It squats like a shipwreck
or a child's just-outsized coffin lifted up
by floodwaters into wrong light,
the quilt chest—my great-grandmother's hold
on what they were and wore in their keeping
from true cold,
in their rolling each morning from under
the pieced, turned-over fields of their lives.
It's too heavy for any room of mine.

The wide lid is one board,
heart of a pine we'd never recognize,
shut now upon nearly nothing,
a faint salt dust only,
flakings from the dreamed-under patterns,
leather-flecks from saved baby shoes,
sweet odor of dead sex, vinegar of sweat,
breath caught
a hundred and fifty years
in this wood's strong current.

Those missing
from photographs, gene-strands, thumbprints,
tinkering spirits,
threads from the absent restless
bedclothes—a leakage unwanted as the light
old fear and love let into hard sleep,
sap from the original
tree it is my own voice saying

green and yellow, whole skies, blue
herons, lilies, rings, glassware, cows,

orchards, pistols, red hats, mayhaws,
the heart's loose change flying.

If you say you would go to that country,
here is the boat and the river.
So the way is pure mourning. So we'll weep!
We'll know everything, weeping for so many,
hearing the huge, deep-starred tree
as it answers us, needle after needle,
with these thick, muddy colors for weather,
these sharp little stitches holding on
across the eyes,
under the breastbone.

One Street

No one speaks of the way
towns shrink in the night,
the world taking them back
bit by little bit.
They give in
the way faces do underground.

Days, our mirage keeps things going.
Only the old people know,
dozing at noon,
how the porch rails soften
and the stairs give up their nails,
the roof sifting down, down
the little speeches of dust.
Only the old people know this,
asleep at all hours,
their breath our shelter.

Front Porch

for Del Marie Rogers

This is deep-roofed shelter
for a roomful of weather,
the first and last of the journey,

and a boundary you can stand on
from inside or outside
without taking a position.

Anything can meet anything
where household touches wider
world in mud-tracks on the floor.

Here, rocking chairs turn back
on what is left of winter,
bent mourners against the housewall.

We've mostly given it up for lost,
made do with a backyard deck at most.
The cost of that is in direction.

But even now, sometimes, you'll hear one
called home,
that sound like nothing but wind

plucking a long wooden swing
whose arms are full of leaves and lamplight,
shadow-trees on the tall steps, climbing.

One Year

Doves sounded the autumn distance early,
and town was a tangled knot among the fields.
It hummed an animal, schoolroom sound.
Blackberries put on their slow dark
near our house. The ripening sun
set tin roofs ablaze all afternoon.
A lame man cut our tall grass with a scythe.
Nothing was the same and everything
was shadows turning the farm around,
deep color simmering just under
the leaf's green water.

Once or twice words jutted from a page,
and some photographs leaked the future
like the foreign light a blow lets in your eyes.
Those moments, my ribs would leap; something
would settle itself, a thin metallic winter
unlike winter, unlike anything,
would come. Of course it didn't come.
Not then. There were people whose skins
I remember the smell of.
They came that close.

Roller Rink

That summer it just appeared,
like a huge canvas butterfly
pinned to McNaughton's field.
All of us half-grown came every day
to watch and try, in love
with unlikely motion, with ourselves
and the obscure brother
who was older and came from a nameless far end
of the county. He knew, from somewhere,
how to do it, the dance of it turning
faster than music, could bend
and glide smooth as a fish where we fell,
could leap, land and roll on
squatting, backward, one-footed.
We loved him for looking blade-boned and frail,
for being always alone with nothing to tell.

In August the old man who'd taken our change
hefted sections of floor and his tent
and his music into a truckbed and left.
The autumn that came after
rose for us with so perfectly clear
a cry of wild geese and amber light
on its early winds, with so many stars
let loose, and leaves in the rain—
even our shambling, hopeless town
seemed good, just in that turn
before the wheel of the year came down.

Of course it never came again.
There was the round brown place
where grass wouldn't grow in that field,

but would grow next year with great ghost wheels
of queen anne's lace.
That summer was a line we'd stumbled over,
and so we were free to fall and gather
the dear, unskillful, amazing losses
departure needs. We took them all,
our bodies shooting crazily
into and through each other. And finally past
to army, city, anyplace far.
We took any road out we could take;
but none of us with the sweet-lifting grace
and ease of the promise that farm boy made
who went and stayed.

Repetition

Lidded three-quarter
moon climbing liveoak's ladder
doubles her face in the owl's mirror.
She is she who called our fathers
waiting by rivershine and twigfire,
wild to gather from wild air
all the fox's dark red feathers.
But fox narrowed and answered never
the old-hearted question in the hunter,
though moonlight spread like blood on water
and the rough crucifix of geese passed over.

Escaped and alone, fox rides the wind's hair,
twists brushfire through the year's weather.
By any river, those footprints flower.
Now *this* moon sings in the tree's fingers,
red-pelted, earth-held flyer,
her names like arrows in the owl's quiver.

What hound's cry rides our dark like a mane of fever?

Lines on a Poet's Face

for Robert Penn Warren

Furrows of the wide brow
are legible as a good field:
what is the name of the world?
Any piece of earth,
even that which becomes in time
a face,
is burial ground
not warned of, and so plowed anyway.

The eye hawk-sure, as when from a hill's crest
live prey is sighted
or, sudden gleaming out of place,
a boy's marble is seen to signal
forfeit in the sun's fingers.
Time is the mirror—
flesh-pockets deepening under the eyes
—into which you stare.
Our grandfathers carried, for coins,
soft purses shaped like this slippage
of years over the socket-bone,
those dense with nonnegotiable
knowledge, memory, cotton-lint stuck to a thin dime
in counties the good rain shunned.

The cheeks' folds run drunk-crooked
as hill roads the storms pulled down
though thought twist starward
into the pure guesswork of joy.
Let likker, like philosophy, roar in the skull.

The ears are heavy with too much
time or music or pain,

which may be all the same thing.
From recall of the nocturnal timbre—
the mouth is drawn now tight
as a trotline to which some river has given
all its leaping and light-scaled syllables
—and the dark wonder.

And still the field burgeons, risen
long past summer,
edges of wild woods pushed, just,
back toward dusk.
We never know what we have lost or what we have found.
October maples brighten and sear
for the young man named for his head afire,
a whisper of stirred water near, snow
coming and the wind
opening its purse where the hawks spend it.

We have undergone ourselves, therefore
what more is to be done for the sake of truth?
Unremarked as the one red kernel
in the yellow handful,
truth falls dark as a blood-spatter
for the sake of its shining, for the sake
of the random crow flying upland,
old Black-and-Glisten, that frazzled call
knocking its fist against sheeted light—
this being one
name for the world
of all the names that are right.

Redlands Journey

What could going back there claim for me
under the generations of trees,
among shadows thrown like dishwater
from the porches that are left?
Rags of red dust spin in those backroads
like the small storms of Sunday children
raised by nothing but wind.

That girl with dark copper hair, her eyes,
even her skin so nearly the color of pennies
I secretly guessed her Indian—she stood
stiller than anyone in the schoolyard's
redbrick sun. Her presence among the stories,
the ones we never told,
is perfect the way one weathered board is
remembered without reason,
a play of surfaces so ordinary
it can only stay.

Like the Latin that stuck to the roof of my mouth,
the double names of tough farm boys are lost,
those torn out by fistfuls from the ground,
rolling and fighting, stained with red, furious clay.
Without shoes,
they taught us to look away.

How far toward them can I see
this way, one letter at a time?
One leaf after another, October
builds a burning tree.
Both a time and a language, this

gathers at my sleeve and skirt hem,
weather, something about to happen

then. As if I walk there now.
As if I have become that wanderer
who walked on time each autumn into town
carrying a sack, pulling a grindstone.
He went through us, nowhere to nowhere,
by the bad backyards of the year,
his feet raising companions of red dust,
the whole town watching his curse.
Household by household, edge by edge,
he put the shining on.

To shamble out of town then, late,
down the old Attoyac road with its moon high.
To damn the sack of pullets, satisfied
with the few coins, the backsteps faces, and the whine
all day of *dull* against the stone,
its sound like red stars.
The turning sings and sings. That's what there is.

You try to shake that clayey dust. It won't
shake. You'll be back.
Nothing wears out.
You'll light old knives and scissors for the dark.

Part

TWO

Mineral

to my mother, 1902–1944

After the nightmare has flown
its white pennant, after the guesswork
is washed from the life of the lost,
still comes a plumbeous shining
I know as yours, dusklike,
winter on a forest floor.
I keep a piece of porous rock
gives off that smell, the furious
permanence you became.

Thirty-five years late, a grief
the child could not have known to know
is yet nothing like grieving, is only
the long diffuse memory of self
staking out first knowledge by absence.
It is the closest I can come
to mourning's reversible gift.

And clearer than any recall, far
clearer than photographs that have curled
around their faces like babies asleep,
is this featureless strength, stone
lit from within and gathering
rootless, terrible shadows close as kin
the way lanternlight does,
making its way in the moonless hour
from houses of the oldest poor.

The Elizabeth Poems

I. *Box-Camera Snapshot*

She stands sharp as a plumb line beside the flowerbeds.
That's July melting the starch in her dress.
Yard dust grits the air, fuzzes the zinnias.

Straw-yellow plaits pulled so tight the eyes slant,
eyes grey as an owl's *who*, she'll wait
among those feral flowers that can grow anywhere.

I can't remember her dream—that ladder
collapsed inside like the skeleton
of some resident starved animal, rib after rib letting go.

She's the one I poke for with sticks,
after the family burials, after the housefires,
in the rubble and smoke of return.

Whose true name couldn't stay, this child's
name nicked and cut back, eked out what is left.
It coats my eyes like ashes or milk.

To see nothing but through this
string figure, lost shoe, puppet broken
out of the play, is less

and more than enough. Out of my hands
the zinnias pop and range, the sun of that year
pumping orange, scarlet, yellow over old ground

nothing should thrive in, the unseen in black-and-white.
She thrives and wears me like a dress. Her speech
is my sleep, all night the colors of loss discovered.

She will have her desire,
whatever that bone was, even love
counting its missing fingers.

II. *Afternoon, Playing on a Bed*

Colored sticks leap from her fingers, settle
among marbles cloudy with rose and yellow.
All of an hour she has tossed and made these
be other, out of her hands.
Bumps on the bedspread have marked her thighs.
She rubs how the skin knows
where it's been.
And the grandfather comes through the screendoor streaming
late sun off his shoulders.
Coming a rain. Heard the east thunder.
She knows there can be no weather
until he tells it.

So the red stick she holds is already old
in what she remembers ahead of her: rain is
the wet chickens huddled in their smell of ashes,
brickwalk washed dark and slick, the cistern
pinging. She is stopped barely hearing
the radio hum its *somewhere
in the Pacific.*

No one she knows is in the places
the radio talks. She is here.
And far back in the house, Grandmother
clinks among pots under the kitchen's one-eye.
Lightbulb on a string sways there and throws
her shadow farther than the rope swing goes.
She thinks that shadow
out the back door all the way to the cows.

Yard-weeds lean away from the wet
that is coming. Sun fades in the screendoor,
nightbugs burring where the light has torn.
She wants—
is it to taste this?
Cooling brick, cistern-tin, pink bedspread,
feather, fire poker, rocker varnished with salt:
her tongue knows how each tastes like itself.
Herself, a mouth on her knuckle.

What is so important that it shuts her throat?

Not even the big marble hurting her knee
can make her move. She is spread
over everything like its own taste
and everything is together the way her toes
are on her feet, her arms on her shoulders,
an ache in all of it, this keeping.

Should she cry? The grandfather's listening
to the Pacific, sighing his pipe into sparks.
This, this, she whispers and waits.
It is only summer, only summer and evening.
But might something fumble and miss?
Might the furniture run away like the dog
or the roof crumple down;
might the hens come loose from their hinges
or the grandfather, grandmother   *mother*
come apart like the handful of sticks?
I will hold on tight. But if I can't,
what is the name of what happens?

She is still as she knows to be, the toys
rocking a little with her breath,
and the hard thunder turns over black

and the clacking marbles are falling.
She remembers the name. *Dead*
is the name she remembers. And wakes
to the drum of the rain
breaking its long sticks in the dark
on the round world rolling.

III.   *Asthma, 1948*

Before dawn, the stick-child
thinned out like a rosebush,
woke crying again. *Hush.*
Accept what the steam kettle offers.
She choked and took in rounds of air.
She gave them back.

Sick days, catalogs kept her quiet.
Hot-colored pages splayed on her bed
bright things that with scissors and paste
could be had.
Nights she dreamed those gold rings
with diamonds like little suns,
her tenth year's skinny finger pointing
         this one   *that one.*

And she floated like a stoppered bottle
on yellow rings of steam from the kettle,
her message, her *no*, rolled tight in the lung-flesh.
She floated and chose one after another
the bright circlets locked up with stones
for fingers and wrists,
for ribcage and neckbone.

IV. *Witness*

Begin with a morning.
I take this one,
its old light, its thin
dusty windows.

Look into the backyard. A woman
is standing on two ends of a broomstick
laid on the neck of a hen.
Bending, she grips the shit-caked feet,
jerks the creature loose from itself.

Flung past its own watching
yellow eye, the near thing soars, hits ground,
and scrabbles again into its one strange flight.
Crossing and recrossing the path
of the child whose blue eye is caught
forever in the skein of this travel,
the hen flops and gathers, flings out
the length of what's left.
There is neither time nor any place to be
until the child can stop looking and hen-eye
can stop and the sun be still on the eggful
of blood laid against fenceboards.

Gone cloudy as butter, the one eye looking up from dirt
will shut down its mirror, though something yet drifts
between it and the other, the wind still
breathing out white down-flowers.

Who hazards what the child might remember
or what its value, the woman gone indoors,
the rest of it

what ruined touch or dance after dark
to dismember and chill again?

I have watched this more than once
from a windowsill wholly dust,
myself stockstill in noon light,
hearing the dove's note lift
the only way it ever does, far off.
Yellow and deep blue, the flags
of summer's flowers were blooming
close to home like the gift of sight.

V. *Fishing*

The rub of that summer warmed her sickroom.
Sticks she gathered with her father
flared in the wind, only blown curtains and fever,
but the picnic fire browned the edge of the dream.
Shadows on the ceiling bloomed
green and speared with sun.
They walked again by the creek
where the fish turned around and came back.

This time the fish are part of the water
moving too fast to be caught,
their bitter silver breaking the nets of light.
Overhead, the summer leaves
clench suddenly and fall.
Her father hands her a stone to hold,
a piece of flint, an arrowhead.
It speaks into her hand:
*this time everything is different and you
have forgotten to bring food.*

VI.   *Traveling, 1950*

for William Stafford

It is winter. We can just glimpse the moon
passing where the trees are gone.
It is miles of farms, my father driving.
In the heater's flannel air, I'm almost dreaming
black cornspikes and fences. It is then

we pass a house so near the road
we're touched with small, sudden light
from the windows, bolts of dim yellow
flung like silk across a broken porch,
a well in the swept narrow yard.

And caught, the blue-checked tablecorner, chairback,
head-and-shoulders shadow in the frame
that will repeat itself for life, still
the only windows lit for—how far
have we gone? I look
until the distance snaps it off.

My hand pressed to icy glass, I feel
how pure necessity can rise
out there like wind, the moon-grayed land become
different under that wind, a story
always to begin.

Some things are so simple they are seen
exactly true just once, and then forever
the pieces in the mind come back
not fitting anywhere,

clear only then
in poor houselight that clouds our car

as if we are the mirror passed
across a face for evidence,
across a sleeping country where some war
has just commenced.

I say it's nothing. I don't speak of it.
My breath on the dark glass leaves a dripping print.

To My Father, Killed in a Hunting Accident

R.L.S., 1904–1974

You'd have been waiting all morning
under the flares of longleaf pine
alone with the gun in your arms.
And watching, as you were always watching.
This was the way trees are
under the sun plain as a hand,
such waiting its own place, without time,
and printed with the squirrel's passage
and the small yellow sounds of grass.
The sky of it was the oldest circle
of hawk and sparrow.

Holding the gun, remembering to think
of holding the gun, you held
a lifetime bent to the minor gods
of a particular and passing kingdom.
Its history waited with you—this light
only daybreak on the first kill you shouldered,
this sun splayed on your great-grandfather's bear.
Did your daydream search those red seasons,
knowing each of their beasts,
fur, hoof and jawbone, for a trophy
you could perfectly own?
Did you think again of that emblem, the knife
you once lost by the muddy Sabine, water rising,
you fourteen and lost too on your pony?
Telling that story, you were always sure
the one blade you needed was back there.

I cannot guess your careless thought,
how it unfolded in pine scent,
some strand of memory or need unwinding

too taut and suddenly
broken just *there* on a buried edge,
your father's father's gun taking on
a weight that shifted utterly
      because of a low branch
rock underfoot or a root
     the stumble because the world does
turn over turn over and kill because
the world does and the sound of it
dies out and dies out
in the hot thick light, and ground
can shake like the hide
of a thing enormously alive.

You got to your feet for hours
holding your opened belly,
cicada-hum braiding through red
pain hope love terror
gripping the backbone.

You were standing when strangers found you.

I who am daughter and stranger
find you in every weather of sleep,
the fox's lent eyes seeing for you,
the will of the gut-shot deer holding on
where the bobcat in darkness brings out
its wreath of claws, and the smoldering
remnant wolf lays a tribal ghost.

I have nothing to give you but this
guesswork and care; oh careful
as the long women who bring wildflowers
to graves in that country, I place
live birds in the hours you stood for.
And to me you have given a history

bearing up its own animal, the alien
close kin and enemy
who eats in my house
now that the weapons are given away.

Poised in any prayer I make for light,
to catch the way it glances off the world,
your ignorant knife is
praising the river, praising
currents of canebrake, pinewoods,
thickets under the wild sky—
whatever lives there lost,
and whatever is helped to die.

Surviving the Wreck

Sometimes in the drift between sleep and waking,
that moment like a great bird calls far back
in the brain's stem where even birth's memory
is intact and sings darkly,
though there is nothing to see
of what paused and flew
when car and bridge, colliding, threw me
out of my fifteenth spring.

After the farm-to-market road
under a muddy night sky, its little rain,
I remember nothing.
               That memory is white
as snow's perfect landscape
shaking every hold and direction loose.
In white bands around the oldest photographs
is something of this:
the captured familiar, then nothing.
What if the sepia grass in stopped wind
went farther, what might wait unremembered
that was, then, part of the rest of the picture?
It *was*. Whatever it was.
And in borders of snow, the hidden print.

The car did strike and go over the bridge
and I out of it went over.

Sometimes the mind tries to unstitch, leaf by leaf,
that tree of scars:
this way the spindle of knowledge let go,
its looped webs crazing the rainy cornfield,
a short life's huge

smashed puzzle scattered thin as weather;
like this bone-splinter rammed out if its packet
felt among weed-roots an earthen wind.

No.
For three days the world
was only absent.

And my life ticked open as the scars banged shut,
the place beyond the pictures edging out
just where the hospital's window faced
a September pasture
                    three bay horses grazed.
There before any waking knowledge
was a river dazzled of grass,
and the light poured on it a river.

Ferried in animal shine so pure it had to wear
the part of pain, first sight
rode creatures edged as blades in what they were.
Like hair-boats set afire, they caught the sun,
establishing clear as any stars
their three directions and the missing one.
And what is firm and what is air—
and time, that language of shadows.

Even this long after,
I can't lose it.
The blank wings pause, drop something,
go on.
        And those three horses come.

Part  THREE

Note for the Birdwatchers of the Sublime

In thin Andean kingdoms, flutes
were made from the wingbones of condors,
breath singing down
the corridors of broken flight.

Well, these years are stacked small,
the daily extinctions
soundless and clean as chickenbones on a plate.
And the wrong shape for luck.
Who was it sailed in a tree,
believing and practicing?

I hunched close to the sky,
cloud-hearted, featherless,
with no knack and no tether,
with no way to get down, and my prayer
that the ground would come closer a failure.
I jumped clean from the chinaberry.

I tell you,
the wind came back like a foreigner,
every breath meaner, every breath darker.

The Farm

Perhaps it comes at night
bearing its own candle.
Or it may come otherwise, to unlight
our daytime task of belief
in the hands' occupations, machines
and their signals, the faces of strangers,
the future that repeats in a metal tray.

It comes the way the earthworm's path
becomes part of the traveling creature,
the way creeks wear down rockbed,
and leaves take up
the empty spaces of April.

Have you seen the shape of young corn at sunset,
a gatepost wound with trumpetvine,
the shovel cast down
near a yardful of hens tocking in last shine
of dusk? There is a step of stone
beside the porch, gourds piled beside it,
those uses gone except for color.

How use for color
the aching back, ashes
of drought-murdered bread,
the grip torn free of an iced-over pump?
These too are part of the fields' speech:
the woman irretrievably mortgaged,
the child weakening, the calf dead,
and the man axing wood who sees
his leg suddenly nothing but blood.

Insubstantial as the whuffing ghosts
that drift above the nostrils of cattle in cold,
it rises from our sleep, a smell like sweat.
No more able to lose this than to lose
mother or father, we disguise it
as everything: freedom, guilt,
ignorance, beauty, oppression,
death, innocence. History.

Melons in my grandfather's field
had always one paler side
from touching earth, remembering that dark
with a little loss.
Melon-shaped, the day moons float,
wafers of fever,
over the feeding cities, the dredged rivers.

A televised scientist can tell us now
that crops will someday grow as far
as stations can be nailed to orbit.
As if enameled artifacts in launchpad wires
will sing some song we know; as if
an armored speculum will yet reflect
only time's old furrow and that rain.

As if the dream sent into flight
could take the nightmare with it.
Losing the singular gift, a little risk
to be born into, against,
we shape a world that will become all risk,
as warfare will become all light.

Until, from necessary dark, we take
the real, pared moon we've earned.
Then, knowing what we ask,

we'll ask the ground again
to dream us if it can.
For now, we flinch and drowse.

We plant geraniums in a trench around the house.

Poetry Workshop in a Maximum Security Reform School

I brought them an armful of apples,
incense, and a branch of autumn leaves.
These children have eaten the incense.
Green dye in the stuff has printed their mouths
and is harmless, though they hate and hope.
They have rolled up the leaves for smoking
and have opened the apples, joking of razorblades.

Greenfaced and sick of the artful
part-time in their time that is whole,
they know any word is the same knife
and that blood is so simple
it only wants to get out.
I say I understand. I do. So I start again
on the scarred blackboard:

   poem   *weapon*

The Clouded Leopards of Cambodia and Viet Nam

They are gone, almost, into the music of their name.
The few that are left
wait high and hesitant as mist
in the tallest trees where dawn breaks first.

Their color of mourning kindles
to patterns of stark white, random
and sudden as hope or a daydream.
Moving, they could be mirrors of the sky,
that play of masks
behind which the ancient burning continues
to dwindle and flee.

Thousands of years in their bones
leap blameless as lightning toward us.
To come close to what they know
would feel like thunder and its silent afterword.
We would turn slowly on our shadows, look up
again to name the shapes of the world:
monkey, temple, rat, rice bowl, god,
images echoed in the smoke of village cookfires,
in the drift of memory on the faces of elders.
We would stand in the clean footprints of animals,
holding like an offering our hope
for the lives of a handful of people,
a rain that is only rain.

Twentieth Anniversary

This is the silence known, a place
like the kitchen of an old, high-ceilinged house
where summer's heat has a layering
coolness as if there were woods
or a river close enough by.
When the woman who uses such a place has gone
out of the body of bread dough into her own,
when the man has walked his way to a porch,
and the child has opened the last door,
there is this.

Crumbs swept from the table
glow in a wedge of sun. As in heaven
or the time before birth,
here there is neither eating nor drinking.
The faucet holds one drop imperceptibly
growing, holds precisely the one note
it will let fall.

And whatever singing, forgetting or nightmare
howled in the house between man and woman,
the child laughing or stifling
in a clenched sleep, here
it is summer and cool, the shelves
green with okra, beans, pears in clear jars.

So clear to each other we see clean through,
we've put away whole pieces of the world
that grew in us. We are this late
quiet light that holds all afternoon,
color of those sharp yellow weedflowers
we look for when the trees begin to bare

the rest of things. Even winter
can wear such still shining,
this pair of rings.

Blind Singer

Her movement's hesitant, close-in, but sure
as if she knew this place but knew it elsewhere.
She never wears, outreaching and unreasonable,
the trust of the always blind. She can remember
what blue distance is and how the shapes of things
are put with light between like membrane.

She plays the local taverns. Her voice
has range and an odd disorder
not quite blues, not quite another thing.
That uncertain edge brings people in,
though she's not graceful under the applause
she knows as a coursing of little stones downhill
or her carpenter grandfather's
bright handful of dropped nails.

And this is most hers: she can't be surprised.
Informed, as madness is, by memory's wild eyes
at windows where only darkness burns,
she sees by turns the world's extremes:
a horse may be a violet, or eggs turn knives,
a dress become a flag, a flag a fire—
the way sleep's rainy mirror lets our lives
become what else they really are.

Still, it isn't dreaming but another
pure combination of consciousness and death,
knowledge without a place to catch, the reel
spinning on and on in the mind's grasp,
the line inexhaustible.

Singing's what she does. And afterward,
in a room with a lit, unnecessary lamp,
she turns a pack of shiny, colored cards.
She turns them all. She turns them all face up.

From the Dunked Clown at the Carnival

Down again, I kept trying to tell you
how the unclear image of my own face
reached from black water I leaned over.
The bright ball and your pitching arm
were only the clever instruments.

Because you thought I hated a drowning,
you kept taking my chances,
helping the crowd shout. My name
in their mouths sounded like *freedom*.

Now I can offer my eyes full of water,
my body that knows how to fall,
oiled hair and webbed fingers,
the keys to this element.

Of course you think you have won.
You have gone.
Now, every night without anyone,
I can drop like a stone straight under
into the cool face that is clearly my future.
One by one, letters of the old marquee
are being mailed to the dark, the new owner.

Luxor

The tour over, we foreigners have gathered
in a cloth shop. One of the Russians is singing.
Two Japanese fiddle with a camera.
The rest of the Americans dicker.
I avoid looking at the flint-eyed incense seller.
Through the doorway, we can just see
a sliver of the Nile.

It is real twice for me,
once for each time I crossed it
in the felucca with bright red sails.
Beyond, the lion-colored desert
resumed its journey toward some significant kingdom.
I had to keep whispering *Nile, Nile,*
like a child who might not remember a name.

Now the sunset grips with gold
the long bones of Karnak.
I turn too quickly and order a garment.
Like a dim flower on the shawl of dusk,
the call to prayer opens, the sound
of belled horses shining at its center.

Tonight I will dream a robe
of red water, lion dust,
of lion water, of gnats dancing,
cloth of time, dancing
heat.

Tomorrow, says the merchant, *tomorrow.*
It is all familiar, this country,
the children like shriveled prayers,
this magnificent
dress of fear and bitter, bitter light.

To Sylvia, Grown Daughter

You who loved so much the creek mud
and the green-shaded woods, all many-
legged moving things, all small hiding
flowers—so like yourself then—
now you are this tall someone
and bright as a fire. Dear lantern!
But listen:

lit with fallen apples and plain grass,
with salamander and birdfeather,
with candles of spring pine,
the old rooms will have waited
the way a forgotten house waits at the edge
of a snapshot you hardly meant to take.
The place has its own moon
and no noise but the cricket's skinny one.

You may enter by the door of what is not yet,
as you did before. Or by the new door
of what has been taken from you.
Pain will let you in, or fury. Ordinary
love will let you in, or any dying.
No key is too odd, no reason too far away.

It is only the house of your first name
that belongs also to the skyful of branches,
to dove, treefrog, and milkweed,
those who begin again.
I say this because it is so simple.
I tell you because it is anyone's,
and because the likeness may be torn
by now. And you may not know.

Topsail Island

January absolves the village.
Summer left no flags. I'm living
just now alone in a room on stilts.
Whatever silts this way is what I've got.

It's clean. Even the fake flowers
left behind on a porch step
are stripped of pretension.
They bloom no-color, original plastic.

Perhaps I am here to practice.

Surely at night these houses break
and sail on perfect silence into the world's
dreams of vacant houses. Then we all move in,
without even a lamp or a suitcase,
until the morning's drydock light
establishes them again, crooked and empty
on their bad knees.

Miles under a blue sun, sand
in my shoes, my heavy parka on:
this is the way the child whispered
I'm the only one.
So many swimmers pulled away from my hands.
Not one of them reached back.
I'm learning the stroke, stroke,
afloat and purposeful along these paths
following a windful of gulls and grackles.

For now, the island's mine, talking
a cold tongue blue,

the light shot with birds.
The stretch of script behind the tide
I've got by heart,
though every day a new translation
lies down in the clarity of salt.

The shells are millions of new doors, all open
to the constellations of fragments.
In the dunes where long grass bends to trace
every tick and tock of wind, the dead
dry fast. Beak and crabclaw hold
what can be held. The tern's dropped flightfeather
knows its own weight at last. Like this
I mean to weather.

Two Words

for Gerald Barrax

Far west of my late afternoon,
mountains I've never seen search California's
sky for snowdrifts. I can only guess
at shapes of trees and flowers
born of such high thrift.
On the flats below, nothing greens.
Rainshadow.
        It is a word for thirst.

In my country, small birds are surging
into October. They gather at dusk,
their pillar of smoke swirling
over the dead chimney,
a dream getting ready to dive,
the fire going backward.
Swifts.
        It is a word for visible wind.

Imagine the lives of such words.
Subtle as the interiors of antique jars,
they shape their enclosed dark
because we hold them to be;
and name after name, they give us the many.

If we should break the clay,
as we can, able to do anything,
believing as we do in no vessel,
believing in fragments, in nothing—
night would step out, the old
wild messenger

51

bearing the same steep shade,
the same configurations of black wings.

Whatever we hoped to say,
it was there all the time.

Part
FOUR

The Swan Story

to Don

but the youngest was left
with a swan's wing instead of
an arm, for one sleeve was
wanting to the shirt of mail.

from "The Wild Swans"
by Hans Christian Andersen

I.

If you take my hand
and what you hold is instead
the prickle and broken
knuckles of feathers, dismantled
fingers of flight,
                    stay with me anyway
where we walk in the year's last snow.
If I tell you only a child's tale,
its fragment of singing, its unkempt
puzzle not worth it,
                    stay.

2.

Once, wisteria grew round
like a cave or a purple room
where I hid to read long afternoons
that tilted the house and barn toward miracle.

Something flew out of the stories,
my eleven years not yet memory
flapping voiceless and spellstruck
over the derelict kingdom, over
the listing farm, pickets and wild grass,
the exiled orchard.

54

Without brother or sister, I wore
all the faces, played sibling
to henyard flocks,
pouring out a teacupful of sand.
In graceless tumble and shit-bloom,
possum-robbed, sad-tailed, the hens
scratched their dotty alphabet in dust.

3.

In the orchard pond, sun looked
at itself through green.
Frogs leaped into flowers
of shattered light.
The dead mother was a black mirror
where my face wouldn't grow,
its other side only pond-silver,
only the known true world
but hidden still, and unwilling.

Night after night,
over sleep's waters burning blue
in their permanent glacial sun,
I flew the changeable journey,
a cradle of feathers under me,
a kinship, a wonder.
Down there, the day-shadows drifted
undone in the sea's glass dance.
Beautiful as fishes, the nightmares to come
were clotting into reefs.

In dream's icy candescence,
the heart knows how to fall
—*that to fall into darkness*
is to be human awhile—
its landmark the rock-shape of loss.

String and tatter, a life
is what it can find
growing wild in woods and churchyard,
houseyard, abandoned orchard.
At the edges where Word *and* Doorsill *die,*
the fieldmouse will stay, and the thrush
under the hawk's eye. The ant will build
at the foot of the apple, and that tree
let down its poor bundles for birds.
There burns the green to be crushed,
to be spun in earth's turn,
the garment our bones wear
weaving itself of humus,
of light the dead are.

Becoming the stung palms of grief.

5.

Possums my father blasted from night's tree
lay flat and stiff on the spread mornings,
flies in their teeth;
and the farm's dog nursed a worm-hole deep
as an eye-socket in the breathing flank,
crossed with bloodless tendon-strings.

How did my mother go
out spark by spark? I could just
remember the box of churchlight,
the strange crowded roses.
I thought she'd left to be
that dun stone angel whose hands were broken off
before I was born into the name it wore.
The whole farm was buried

under a grainy light, the necessary
word sinking deeper, and the missing
hands of the stone.

The pantry's vegetable years
dimmed in their jars;
the milk pan glowed like a downed moon
and the wine darkened,
hissing its way up.
On the dark parlor table, a blown glass swan
lifted clear wings, a flight of rain.

6.

Mornings after storms I watched the light
tip its arrows in every brier and bush,
even the possum with his bloody smile,
even the dog eaten down to the bone
and the grave stone clear across town
shining.

Nettle, thorn and sandspur,
the world stings itself into summer.
It can open the hands like stars.

Already the future was threading
green fires. I would startle forward
like the hens shoved out of silence
by the predator's pink bright eye.

7.

From love to death to love
spirit in a splintering bone-cart
jounces, rags and tangled hair,
in silence

always toward the last fire;
and still with its green-burnt hands
weaves.

When the bird—for rescue—alights
like flurries of white air, like snow,
when the body's yet-wanting green
is flung over that whirling flight,
O makeshift forever—
dry sticks piled for a killing flame
will burst, every time, into blossom.

8.

Broken then
from the heat-blister of childhood
into fragrance of snowrose and firerose
bud and thorn-nub stirring in flesh
ready to crave and go out,
I woke to no kin but myself
of the long making.
All the winged brothers were folded
under my own skin,
this unfinished shift all I'd have on my back
for the rest of my left-handed life;
all I'd have in one hand this
web, quill and featherbone
to shadow my path with a draggled trace
like a one-sided angel in snow.

Then was the dog unstrung, gone up
like a kite, the worm
blown out of its tunnel.
The hens rose straight out of their tracks.
Tooth by tooth, the possum let go of his grin.
And the stone took up her hands of earth.

9.

Long ago the sky came down,
pond water full of refracted birds,
and the grounded kingdom lifted its heavy wings.
In the dark mirror whose face I know,
my mother's hands become a stand of simple weeds.

10.

If this is a story, it ends here,
halfway to knowing how.

Only the earliest dream is hollow
and sings. Only that reed
is not filled. Wise bone, flute,
it breathes old stories
into the savage wind that never closes.

Love, tonight we walk in snow
where the creek is nettled with ice.
It grumbles and clinks
beneath a slick suburban moon.
Under flurries that break like pigeons from the pines,
we are freezing and following
rabbit tracks in the blue shadows.
We will laugh our way home, our bodies ready
to clothe each other with hands.

11.

What are you and I
but the one dreamed story
that out of time breaks into many?

We walk toward our winter fire
under the sky's downfall,
Bird-Loose-Feather whitening our hair.
Dear one, hold on. We are
only halfway there.